I0819730

The Kind of Noise Worth Writing Down

The Kind of Noise Worth Writing Down

Poems by

Richard LeDue

© 2021 Richard LeDue. All rights reserved.
This material may not be reproduced in any form, published,
reprinted, recorded, performed, broadcast,
rewritten or redistributed without
the explicit permission of Richard LeDue.
All such actions are strictly prohibited by law.

Cover design by Shay Culligan
Cover Photo by Ray Zhou on Unsplash.com

ISBN: 978-1-63980-060-5

Kelsay Books
502 South 1040 East, A-119
American Fork, Utah 84003
Kelsaybooks.com

For Ramsey,
who made me realize the inadequacies of words

Acknowledgments

Rue Scribe: “Music Lover”

Free Verse Revolution: “Transcendence While Working for Minimum Wage”

433: “It Eventually Flew Away”

Distance Yearning: “After Five Weeks of Looking Out The Same Window,” “Sleeping With the Lights On”

Minute Magazine: “One morning”

Mark Literary Review: “Because We Couldn’t Afford Fireworks,” “Disconnected”

Nightingale and Sparrow: “What’s Left in the Cooler”

Mineral Lit Magazine: “My Parents Still Pray”

Thorn Literary Magazine: “Like Lightning in a Night Sky”

Eunoia Review: “Homemade Absolution”

Boston Literary Magazine: “Love Can Live Outside of Words”

Contents

Early Nights and Mornings

The silence of a closed door
at 9 PM
helps dreams flourish,
until forgotten while an alarm clock
barks at 6 AM—
the neighbour's dog outside all night
howling,
as if it knew something
we didn't.

Music Lover

Never learned to play a musical instrument
like a drum in a marching band,
wasn't good at following others
around, timing steps and beats
together, plus my parents were
lower middle class (a nice way
of saying "poor,"), so we couldn't
afford live music, even had to dub cassettes
borrowed from my mother's friends.
Took us a while to catch up
to CDs. Now, my child dances
instead of talking (made it to
upper-middle class, which means
there's enough money to keep
bill collectors from calling,
and songs on my phone paid for
by a credit card that'll take
eighty-some years to repay),
and his words few and out of context,
but reminds me that some of the best music
requires no lyrics.

The Kind of Noise Worth Writing Down

Sometimes a single word
takes a page worth of effort,
while lips go silent
as an unloaded gun,
left to dust
inside a closet, next to a shoebox
of photos too forgotten to even fade,
and we believe we're working towards an explosion,
when really almost everyone's defective
firecrackers, burning down to nothing-
the quiet grey sky
thunderless, but reassuring us
that that won't always be the way.

Transcendence While Working for Minimum Wage

Always stayed up too late,
even when I had to walk to Sunday School
the next day in a snowstorm.
My First Communion was that spring:
got a certificate,
learned little except how god felt
like a course we had to pass.

Much later in life,
at a summer job in a library,
I found answers in the long silences,
realized that oblivion doesn't need
to be shushed, overdue books
mean nothing to the dead,
and the darkness under our eyes
offered us the greatest rest.

My Parents Still Pray

The first time I ate a communion wafer
I was disappointed by the taste,
expected something stronger
or sweet enough to trick me
into wanting more.
I started to let it sit on my tongue,
slowly dissolving
until there was nothing left.
My mouth dry and empty,
while sitting in the back of a car
that never worked right
and would become our excuse
to stop attending Sunday Mass.

Because We Couldn't Afford Fireworks

Shot the Christmas lights out of a birch tree
one New Year's Eve. Glass falling
like heavy snowflakes, silence louder
afterward. My father's rifle
weighed against my adolescent hands,
was actually scared to pull the trigger,
feel the jolt into my shoulder, teaching me
the pain that comes with power.
Can't decide if we were a one gun
salute, or firing towards a sky
where my Sunday school god lived,
immortal on his thrown, grey beard
symbolic of a mastery over tigers and
lambs. Neighbours called the police,
officer relieved we were done by the
time he arrived, joked about the noise,
how people were in bed as if sleep
had more right than sound, dreams
forgotten in morning light more valuable
than the smell of gunpowder on a winter night.

Nothing Stolen, but Something Lost

Someone tried to sneak in our front door
years ago, while I was at school,
learning about something I've long forgotten.

My mother was peeling potatoes
for supper and said "Hello,"
hoping it was me, but there was no answer,
so she gripped the knife tighter
expecting the worse,
only to get the squeak of the door
whispering a surrender.

We'll never know who it was,
but afterward, we always locked the doors
and peeked out a window before answering.

Disconnected

The cable TV was cut off more than once,
yet there was always mashed potatoes for supper
and enough tea bags for the month
(milk bought with my mother's tips),
while I studied for a test.
School was one of the few things I was good at,
as I dreamed of moving to Vancouver
(the weather always seemed nicer there
when I watched the news
on one of the two channels we got
by manipulating coat hanger rabbit ears),
with no bill collectors calling,
insisting I write down a phone number-
their disgust that someone in debt had children
loud enough to make me turn off the ringer
on my own phone, when I finally did move away,
but I never made it as far as I thought I would.

To an Uncle I Never Met

Trains have always seemed too loud
to me. Is that because of you
and your untied shoe?

My grandfather's distrust of white coats
inherited: my blood pressure goes up
in any hospital
(nurse's smile sharp as a scalpel
stuck in my back
before I was even born).

Find it scary how my father's voice
lives in my own
sometimes.

No way to know if I sound like you though.

Your grave unmarked because there were still six
other children who needed to eat.

Your accidental fall onto tracks, under wheels,
created a thunderous silence,
and left me double knotting
my child's shoelaces.

One Morning

brain popping
like firecrackers in a backyard
(my father had one put down his shirt
by his friends when he was a child),
sipping my second coffee
as streaks of light sneaked in
the Venetian blinds on the basement window,
and it was then; I thought I heard god,
the same way you listen to neighbours
upstairs, getting ready for work,
turning off the radio.
Years later, Sunday at 9:31 AM,
that same voice returned,
while I changed my five year old's
diaper, moved my toes, gone cold
from too many windows left open
overnight, hoped my wife's migraine
dissipated by lunch, only to realize
I'd been talking to myself all along.

Seven Hundred Poems

I could write you seven hundred poems.

Some about birds that abandon souls,
or how love says it can fly
without feathers,
but only one would tell of that crow,
who sneaked into our basement:

wings working at something few of us know
could end with noises in the furnace room,
flapping silenced with a BB gun
and lies that it was all handled humanely.

After Five Weeks of Looking Out the Same Window

Snowflakes no longer dance,
but drop blindly
like a prisoner after the firing squad
extinguishes his last cigarette,
and I worry who'll fall upon the blades
of grass next. Bird's song turned
into a lullaby, sleep darker
than a burned out match,
flicked aside.

It Eventually Flew Away

A bird flew into my living room window.
Too small to break the glass,
it had no choice
but to land after the crash,
quivering,
waiting to die,
probably just as dumbfounded
as the rest of us
by current circumstances.

The neighbour's cat nowhere
close, reminding me
how death doesn't need legs,
or even teeth,
but just a cloudy Thursday,
when we believe the chances of rain
the most important thing
to talk about.

Rivaling Silence

The sound of when you're trying
to make no noise,
(curtains closed on another night)
until your sneeze echoes,
yet wakes no one.
It makes you feel like a vampire
alone in the darkness
while staring into a mirror,
wondering where all the light went.

What's Left in the Cooler

The radio plays over the speakers
sometimes at the local supermarket.
Music narrating our frozen green beans,
canned tuna, 100% whole wheat bread,
as if a song can make us forget
too many crave nutrients more than love.
The way some of us clog up the aisle
reminds me of a hunger,
but not for a lover's lips;
that is left to movie stars,
who probably pay someone else
to buy their groceries.
Then there are the poets, who make
their lists into poems about what's left
in the cooler next to the ice cream
and how there was already silence
long before anyone turned off the radio

I hope

an unread poem makes some noise,
even if it sounds like a plastic grocery bag
dancing in an autumn breeze,
only to end up buried
in snow, and disposed of
in the spring.

And summer rain can be the applause
we believe we need to hear.

Wrapped in Silence

There was no news,
meaning everything was fine-
the ice cracked but wouldn't break
today, while supper plates clanged together
in soapy water. Tomorrow,
we'd planned on staying home,
wrapped in silence
as snow quietly filled in our footprints.

Nothing New

Suppose to thunder today:
sky gray leaves turned over
like a cliché with nothing else
to say—light filtering
through the clouds,
competing with lightning,
but no angels battling with laser swords
so we'll close the curtains,
hope the night clear,
quiet,
so we can be alone
with our dreams.

Like Lightning in a Night Sky

Another thunderstorm headache,
sinuses feel like they're bowling,
while the doctor calmly writes
a prescription for pills
I can't pronounce,
she says they *should* help.

I almost hope they're a placebo,
that I'm part of some secret study—
my expertise in pain finally recognized,
impossible to miss,
like lightning in the night sky.

Sleeping with the Lights On

The walls collaborate with the silence
in between every cough turned
into claps of thunder,
flickering lamp in the corner
the only lightning;
desperate for a new bulb
(a package bought three weeks ago
just before the symptoms started),
but there's no Zeus
aiming the bolt to right a wrong
or express his divine rage,
only an electric bill overdue.

Another Abandoned Dream Journal

Another morning condemned
by an alarm clock.
In my sleep, a lightning bolt
barely missed me,
but killed everyone standing on the ground,
while I sat on a table.

My imaginary survivor guilt
snored contently the rest of the night.

A dreamed apocalypse
proving nothing
except how clouds have bad aim,
and precision best left to watch-makers,
who construct tiny hands-
the loudest noise
some nights.

Never Loud Enough

Thunder will always try to be louder than us—
regardless how wide we leave the windows
open at night
or how hard the dishes smash against each other
in an overfilled sink,
it thinks we have already lost.

Regardless of plates thrown against kitchen walls,
or insults hurled with greater precision,
it roars like victory.

Even though deathbed confessions will be whispered
until flat-line beeps
and a loved one wails,
clouds will still gather in triumph,
as thunder fails at being louder than us.

Homemade Absolution

A slammed door
reminds you how loneliness
is more than just being by yourself.
It's those silences
after arguments about socks left on the floor,
dishes only washed after using the last fork,
TV too loud, apologies too quiet,
Valentine roses always bought the next day
on clearance,
but kissed lips allow more forgiveness
than any words-
goosebumps like the first time
you spoke to each other.

Love Can Live Outside of Words

Watching you smash your head
against the wall, and I can only
sympathize, try to remember being
five, imagine still speaking
in gibberish, wearing diapers,
yet knowing I was seduced by words.
Allowed the noises I still make
to flirt with meaning,
until realizing language is a loveless marriage.

Checking your forehead for bruises,
and inside my clenched mouth,
I taste sorrow,
its flavour similar to my own blood.
Being too polite to spit
into a napkin, I swallow it.
Then you grab my hand, needing
something I'll guess at, waiting
for your smile to answer me—
the sentences on this page can't help
but be jealous of their own
inadequacies.

About the Author

Richard LeDue was born in Sydney, Nova Scotia, Canada, but currently lives in Norway House, Manitoba, with his wife and son. He has taught English there since 2009 and especially loves including poetry in his lessons. In 2017, he rediscovered his love for writing poems, which led him to make a New Year's Resolution in 2018 to send out at least one poetry submission a month. This decision helped him to become a published poet. His poems have appeared in various publications since 2019. His first chapbook, *The Loneliest Age,* was released in 2020 from Kelsay Books. His second chapbook, *Winnipeg Vacation,* was released in 2021 from Alien Buddha Press. *The Kind of Noise Worth Writing Down* is his third chapbook.

www.ingramcontent.com/pod-product-compliance
Lightning Source LLC
LaVergne TN
LVHW051023080826
845145LV00009B/2774
* 9 7 8 1 6 3 9 8 0 0 6 0 5 *